Contents

What do trucks do?

You can see lots of trucks on the road. Trucks carry things from place to place.

KINGFISHER
READERS

2

Trucks

KINGFISHER

First published 2013 by Kingfisher
an imprint of Macmillan Children's Books
20 New Wharf Road, London N1 9RR
Associated companies throughout the world
www.panmacmillan.com

Series editor: Heather Morris
Literacy consultant: Hilary Horton

ISBN: 978-0-7534-4099-5

9 8 7 6 5 4 3 2 1

1TR/0516/WKT/UG/105MA

A CIP catalogue record for this book is available from the British Library.

Printed in China

Picture credits
The Publisher would like to thank the following for permission to reproduce their material.
Top = t; Bottom = b; Centre = c; Left = l; Right = r
Cover Shutterstock (SS)/Konstantin Sutyagin; Pages 4-5 SS/Fernando Rodrigues; 6 SS/Christina Richards;
7t Bob Langrish; 7b SS/Cathleen A Clapper; 8 SS/Sergio Schnitzler; 9t Shutterstock/Steve Estvanik;
9b Shutterstock/Dmitry Kalinovsky; 10t Shutterstock/Stephen Mahar; 10-11 SS/Robert Pernell; 11 Corbis/Alvis
Upitis/AgStock Images; 12 SS/R Carner; 12-13 SS/Michail Kabaovitch; 14 SS/Orientaly; 15 SS/Orientaly;
16 SS/abutyrin; 17 Photolibrary/Imagebroker; 18 SS/Dimitry Kalinovsky; 19 SS/Stephen Mcsweeny;
20 SS/Marafona; 21 SS/Marafona; 22t SS/Bram van Broekhoven; 22b SS/Florin C; 23 SS/Sergey Kozoderov;
24 Photolibrary/Tom Brakefield; 25t SS/Daniel Goodchild; 25b iStock/Sun Chan; 26 SS/Mike Brake;
27 SS/Mike Brake; 28 SS/Alexander Chelmodeev; 29 SS/GTibbetts; 30–31 Alamy/Don Hammond/Design Pics
Inc.; 31 SS/mashe

Delivery trucks carry things to the shops for us to buy.

Other trucks do special jobs. How many different trucks can you think of?

Loading trucks

This truck is called a removal van. People load their things into a van like this when they move house.

What are the men loading on to this truck?

This truck is called a horsebox.
It takes horses from place to place.

These horses
are loaded.
Soon they will
be ready to go.

Big loads

What is this truck carrying?
It carries cars from the **factory**,
where they were made. It is called
a car transporter.

How many cars can you see?

This big truck is taking logs from the forest to make into paper.

This **forklift truck** is lifting a big load.

Tankers

Trucks that carry liquids, like oil, water or milk, are round like this.

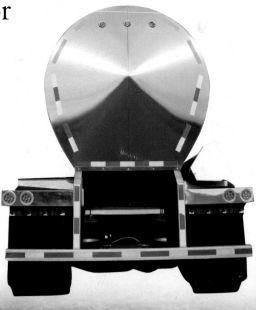

These trucks are called tankers.

This tanker is collecting milk from a farm.

Being a driver

What is it like being a truck driver?

It feels free and easy to be out on the road. On a long journey, the driver parks the truck at night and sleeps in the cab.

But it can be difficult, too. It is hard to drive in bad weather, like rain or snow. Sometimes there are accidents. It can be dangerous on the road.

Farm trucks

On the farm, you see **tractors** doing all kinds of jobs.

This tractor is helping to break up the earth. Then the farmer plants the corn.

This truck is called a combine harvester. It cuts the corn and takes the grain from the stalks.

Why do you think the driver's window is so big?

Mines and quarries

Coal is **mined** from the ground. Big trucks carry the coal away.

A **crane** is loading coal on to this truck. See how big the wheels are!

Big trucks dig rocks from the ground. This truck is in a **quarry**.

Building sites

There are lots of different trucks on a building site. This one is a digger. It has a big bucket on the front. It digs up earth from the ground using the bucket.

Bulldozers push the earth around. This bulldozer does not have wheels. It has a caterpillar tread instead.

How does the caterpillar tread help the bulldozer move?

Dumper trucks

This is a dumper truck. It carries big loads to and from building sites.

The driver tips the back of the dumper to empty its load.

Making buildings

Buildings are made
with lots of concrete.
The concrete
comes to the
building site in
a concrete mixer.

To make a high building, you need a crane to lift things to the top floor.

This crane comes on a truck. It costs a lot to have a crane for a day.

Around the town

As you go around the town, you see lots of different trucks doing jobs to help us.

This is a road sweeper. It helps keep the streets clean.

This is a rubbish truck. It takes rubbish from our bins on the street.

This truck takes rubbish for **recycling**.

Fire engines

This is a very special truck, called
a **fire engine**.

Fire engines carry firefighters,
hoses, ladders, axes and lots of
other things to help put out a fire.

On the roads

When a road gets old, it needs new **tarmac**. This roadroller makes the tarmac flat. It is very heavy and rolls along very slowly.

When it snows, we need
snowploughs to clear the roads.
Then the delivery trucks can get
our food to the shops!

Which truck?

Which kind of truck would you like to drive?

Would you prefer to drive a delivery truck, and be out on the open road?

Or would it be a big construction truck on a building site?
You choose!

Glossary

crane a machine that lifts things up high

delivery taking goods from one place to another

factory a place where things are made

fire engine a truck that helps put out fires with water

forklift truck a truck that picks up heavy loads with two prongs

mined dug from the ground

quarry a place where rocks are dug from the ground

recycling using again

snowplough a truck that clears the snow

tarmac material on the top of roads

tractor a farm truck